PAPER ART
SKILLS LAB

SANDEE EWASIUK

CRABTREE
PUBLISHING COMPANY
WWW.CRABTREEBOOKS.COM

ART SKILLS LAB

Author
Sandee Ewasiuk

Editors
Marcia Abramson,
Kathy Middleton

Photo research
Melissa McClellan

Cover/Interior Design
T.J. Choleva

Proofreader
Crystal Sikkens

**Production coordinator
and Prepress technician**
Tammy McGarr

Print coordinator
Katherine Berti

Developed and produced for
Crabtree Publishing by
BlueApple*Works* Inc.

Consultant
Trevor Hodgson
Fine artist and former director of The Dundas Valley School of Art

Art & Photographs
Shutterstock.com: © passion artist (cover top) © Excellent backgrounds
(background); © AnastasiaNi (p. 5 top right); © rodimov (p. 5 middle right); ©
LaineN (p. 5 top left); © Monkey Business Images (p. 5 bottom left); © Pj Aun
(p.6 top left); © Gilmanshin (p.6 top middle); © Nor Gal (p. 6 top middle right);
© Africa Studio (p. 6 top right); © Banana Republic images (p. 6 middle left); ©
Aigars Reinholds (p. 6 bottom left); © NikolayN (p. 6 bottom middle); © taweesak
thiprod (p. 6 bottom right); © Anton Starikov (p. 7 bottom left); © OlegDoroshin
(p. 7 top right); © Comaniciu Dan (p. 7 middle right); © Sunset Paper (p. 7 bottom
right); © Juriah Mosin (p. 9 bottom left); © DT Creations (p. 17 right); © spatuletail
(p. 21 right);

Instructive paper art © Sandee Ewasiuk cover, p. 7– 29 excluding bios

p. 4 right Kurt Schwitters, Centre Georges Pompidou/Public Domain

p. 5 bottom right © Calvin Nicholls. Reprinted with permission.

p. 11 © Maud Vantours. Reprinted with permission.

p. 15 © Yulia Brodskaya. Reprinted with permission.

p. 19 © Larissa Nowicki. Reprinted with permission.

p. 23 © Kris Grover.(krisgrover.com) Reprinted with permission.

p. 27 © Ann Wood. Reprinted with permission.

Library and Archives Canada Cataloguing in Publication

Title: Paper art skills lab / Sandee Ewasiuk.
Names: Ewasiuk, Sandee, author.
Series: Art skills lab.
Description: Series statement: Art skills lab | Includes index.
Identifiers: Canadiana (print) 20200151533 |
  Canadiana (ebook) 20200151541 |
  ISBN 9780778768449 (hardcover) |
  ISBN 9780778768487 (softcover) |
  ISBN 9781427124302 (HTML)
Subjects: LCSH: Paper work—Juvenile literature. |
  LCSH: Handicraft—Juvenile literature.
Classification: LCC TT870 .E93 2020 | DDC j745.54—dc23

Library of Congress Cataloging-in-Publication Data

Names: Ewasiuk, Sandee, author.
Title: Paper art skills lab / Sandee Ewasiuk.
Description: New York : Crabtree Publishing Company, 2020. |
  Series: Art skills lab | Includes index.
Identifiers: LCCN 2019057506 (print) | LCCN 2019057507 (ebook)
  ISBN 9780778768449 (hardcover) |
  ISBN 9780778768487 (paperback) |
  ISBN 9781427124302 (ebook)
Subjects: LCSH: Paper art--Juvenile literature.
Classification: LCC TT870 .E93 2020 (print) | LCC TT870 (ebook)
  | DDC 745.54--dc23
LC record available at https://lccn.loc.gov/2019057506
LC ebook record available at https://lccn.loc.gov/2019057507

Crabtree Publishing Company

www.crabtreebooks.com   1-800-387-7650

Printed in the U.S.A./032020/CG20200127

**Published in Canada
Crabtree Publishing**
616 Welland Ave.
St. Catharines, Ontario
L2M 5V6

**Published in the United States
Crabtree Publishing**
PMB 59051
350 Fifth Avenue, 59th Floor
New York, New York 10118

**Published in the United Kingdom
Crabtree Publishing**
Maritime House
Basin Road North, Hove
BN41 1WR

**Published in Australia
Crabtree Publishing**
Unit 3 – 5 Currumbin Court
Capalaba
QLD 4157

CONTENTS

GET INTO PAPER ARTS

Approach this book with a sense of adventure! It is designed to discover and unleash the creativity that exists within you. The projects in this book will help you to express your feelings, your thoughts, and your ideas through your art. Create images of things you want to say, and messages you want to share. When learning to create paper art, enjoy the process and don't worry too much about the finished product. Find your own individual style and run with it!

MINI-BIOGRAPHIES

Throughout the book you will find mini-biographies highlighting the work of artists who work with paper. We can learn a great deal about paper techniques by looking at art others have created. Experiment with the techniques they used. Examine the artworks to see how they were composed, or put together, and how **symmetry**, lines, and color were used.

WHAT IS PAPER ART?

A lot of arts and crafts use paper, but they are not all considered paper arts. Paper art transforms the paper by cutting, bending, folding, curving, layering, weaving, taping, and gluing.

Paper art began in ancient China, where paper was invented, then spread all over the world. Many cultures developed their own traditional paper art.

Today, there are different papers for many types of paper art. Paper can be thin or thick or anywhere in between! Cardboard, card stock, and construction paper are sturdy and popular for art projects.

Das Undbild, 1919, Staatsgalerie Stuttgart

German artist Kurt Schwitters (1897-1948) made collages out of found objects and all kinds of paper. He used newsprint, magazines, poems, and even bus tickets.

MAIN TYPES OF PAPER ART

Paper art can fall into one of many categories:

FOLDING

Paper can be folded to create art. Origami is the Japanese art of folding paper. There can be more than 30 intricate folds in one piece. Many other paper arts make use of folding paper as well.

Folding origami

CUTTING

Paper cutting is making a design in a sheet of paper with scissors or a knife. If you have folded a sheet of paper and cut out a snowflake, you've done a simple form of paper cutting. Many different styles of fancy paper cutting can be found all over the world.

Cutting paper

Gluing collage pieces

PASTING

Many kinds of art can be created by pasting or gluing paper to other paper or to a base. These are flat, **two-dimensional** pieces of art. People learned to make glue from natural materials in prehistoric times--long before the invention of paper!

Assembling a paper sculpture

ASSEMBLAGE

Three-dimensional (3-D) art can be constructed by joining paper together using glue, tape, or any type of fastener. The word *assemblage* is actually a French word meaning "putting or gathering things together."

CALVIN NICHOLLS

Canada

Calvin Nicholls combines his love for both art and wildlife in his paper sculptures. He began making them after realizing he could create a bird's layers of feathers with layers of paper. He hand-cuts hundreds of pieces of paper, then glues them together to make the fur and feathers of his wildlife art. Not only are his sculptures very real-looking, he has his critters jumping out of the frame!

White Wolf by Calvin Nicholls

MATERIALS AND DESIGN

You can make many of the paper art projects in this book with thin origami paper, as well as thicker construction paper and card stock. Some of the projects in this book can be made with recycled materials found around the house. Collect paper, old books, and magazines. You will also need paint, glue, and scissors.

Paper can be painted with watercolor paint, acrylic paint, and tempera paint before being made into paper art.

White glue that dries clear and a glue stick work great for collages.

Use a brush to spread glue over a large area.

Old magazines

Maps from old books

Scissors

WHAT SURFACE TO CREATE ON?
You can use a variety of different materials for the background of some of your paper art. Start with any of these examples: canvas board, watercolor paper, or cardboard. In this book, backgrounds will be called art boards, but you can use any of the surfaces. Experiment with different backgrounds, but remember to make sure your surface will support your creation. For example, collage needs sturdy paper as a base or it will wrinkle and buckle.

Canvas boards are inexpensive and come in many sizes. They are a good surface for collage.

Watercolor paper is strong enough to have other paper glued to it and not buckle.

Types of Paper

There are many types of paper used for the paper art projects in this book. The paper listed works best, but you can substitute construction paper for origami or card stock paper.

Construction Paper

Construction paper is made from wood pulp. The surface is not smooth. You can even see small pieces of pulp in it. Though it feels heavy, construction paper is not very long-lasting. It is often used for school projects.

Origami Paper

Thin paper that folds easily is used for *origami*, which is the Japanese word for paper folding. It can be a single color all the way through or it may have a printed design on one side. Origami paper usually comes in squares.

Card Stock Paper

Card stock is a type of paper that is thicker and heavier than regular paper. It comes in many colors and **textures**. Playing cards, postcards, and greeting cards are made with this type of paper. That is how it got its name.

Heavy Plain Paper

Heavier paper works best for painting. Paint is wet and may wrinkle thin paper. Watercolor and sketchbook paper are often used for painting.

Design Elements When Making Paper Art

What makes a work of art good? It will depend on how well the artist has used the elements of design: **line**, **shape**, **pattern**, and **composition**.

Line is the edge between two colors or shapes. It does not have to be straight. Lines can go in any direction and come in any shape, length, or thickness. Artists use lines to draw the viewer's eye in the direction they want it to go.

Shape is any enclosed space in art. A shape's edges may be created by lines, textures, or colors.

Pattern is the way colors or shapes are combined and repeated to create a special effect, such as **contrast** or movement.

Composition is the arrangement of all the shapes, lines, colors, spaces, and textures in an image. Artists carefully place these elements so that the viewers' eyes will follow a path leading to the key element or message of the work.

POSITIVE AND NEGATIVE

Positive space in art is usually the main subject of the artwork. Negative space is usually the background surrounding the subject. You need both to create a piece of art. Negative space makes the subject stand out. Artists often balance the amount of positive and negative space.

You Will Need:

- Construction paper
- Scissors
- Glue stick

PROJECT GUIDES

1. Fold a piece of light-colored construction paper in half. Cut it down the fold line. Set one half aside. Draw **geometric** shapes from the edges toward the center of the paper.

2. Cut out the shapes you have drawn. Save the cut-outs.

3. Use a glue stick to stick the largest cut-out to the center of a black piece of construction paper. Glue the other cut-out pieces around it, putting each one opposite the spot where it was cut out.

4. Find two colors of construction paper, one that is light and one that is dark. Fold the light-colored paper in half. Cut it down the fold line. Set one half aside. Draw shapes that are not geometric from one edge toward the center of the paper.

5. Cut out the shapes you have drawn. Save the cut-outs.

6. Use a glue stick to stick the largest part to the left side of the dark paper. Glue the cut-out pieces so that they are a **mirror image** of the areas they were cut from.

4

5

6

Try This!

The negative space element of art may not be the first thing to jump out at the viewer, but once seen, it becomes an important part of the design. For example, the image at left could be seen as vases—or two ladies! If you see the vases, then you see the white areas as the positive space. The dark areas become the negative space. If you see two ladies, then you see the dark areas as the positive space and the white areas as the negative space.

COLORS IN LAYERS

Layers of paper can be glued together to create a piece of art. By cutting **organic**, or non-geometric, shapes out of sheets of paper and then layering the pieces from light to dark, you can create the illusion of depth. It will look three-dimensional even though it is a flat surface. The center point must be the lightest color to create the illusion. The **overlapping** layers also contribute to the illusion.

You Will Need:

- Card stock or construction paper
- Pencil
- Scissors
- Glue stick

PROJECT GUIDES

1 Select pieces of card stock or construction paper or a mix of both. Make sure to have a range of colors including light and dark colors.

2 Take the second-lightest color piece and gently fold it in half, but don't make a crease. Use scissors to cut a slit in the middle.

3 Unfold the paper. Working outward from the slit, cut a small organic shape.

4 Place the paper with the cut-out shape on top of the next piece of paper. Line up the edges of the two sheets. Use a pencil to trace around the cut shape.

5 Repeat steps two and three with this piece of paper. Use the traced shape as a guide and cut the next shape a bit bigger than the traced shape.

6 Repeat steps two, three, and four with the rest of the pieces of paper. The shapes will get gradually bigger with each piece you cut.

7 Place your sheets in a stack and turn the stack over. The smallest-cut shape will now be on top. Use a glue stick to glue the first sheet to the lightest color of paper, which will have no cut shape. Continue gluing each piece until the piece with the largest shape cut out is on top.

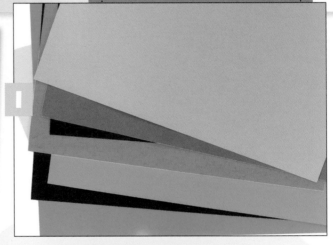

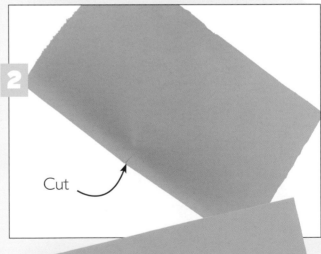

Cut

4

5

6

7

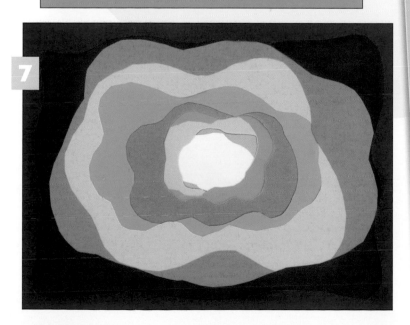

France

As a child, Maud Vantours dreamed about being an artist when she grew up. Today she is one of the most successful paper artists. Vantours uses paper to sculpt three-dimensional works of art. Her creations often look like dream landscapes or cloudscapes. Once she has an idea, she starts by making a two-dimensional pattern. Then she chooses the colors and textures of paper she will use. The final step is cutting and adding layer after layer in different colors and shapes. "I've worked with paper for a long time and there is always a new way to use it," she says. Her work appears in advertisements, magazines, and art galleries.

Landscape, 2017

PAPER MANDALA

A mandala is an ancient Asian symbol that represents the universe and the circle of life. Mandala design can be simple or very detailed. In this exercise, you will create a geometric pattern of folded triangles of paper.

PROJECT GUIDES

1. Use scissors to cut about 30 squares of origami paper. They should be 3 inches (7.6 cm) square. If you have 6 inch (15.25 cm) paper, you can fold each sheet into fours and cut along the fold lines.

2. Fold one of the squares in half. Crease the fold.

3. Fold the paper in half again and crease.

4. Unfold the paper. Bring the bottom left corner up toward the top edge. The point of the corner should meet the top of the crease. Press down and crease the edge. Repeat for the other side.

5. Follow steps two to four on all the other squares you have cut.

6. Draw a circle on a piece of card stock. Draw two **perpendicular** lines through the middle. You will now have four equal quarters. Fill one quarter with triangles. Glue each one down with a glue stick.

7. Duplicate the pattern you created in the other three quarters. Repeating the pattern in each quarter creates what is known as radial balance in the circle.

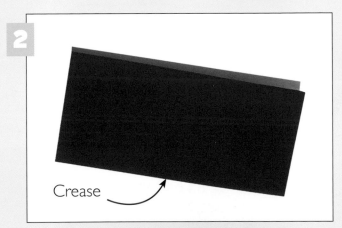

Crease

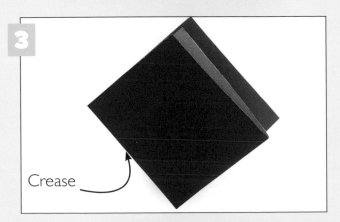

Crease

4

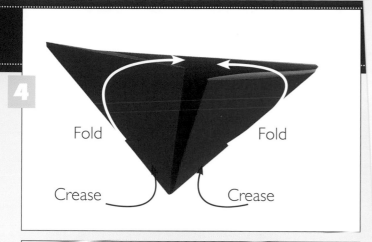

Fold · Fold

Crease · Crease

5

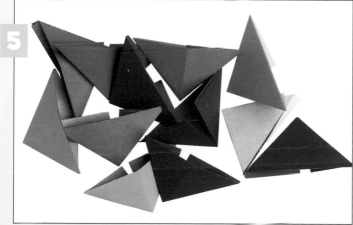

6

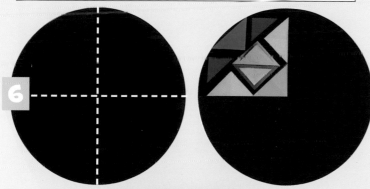

7

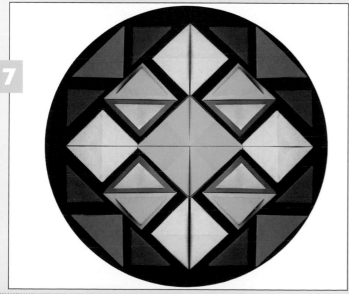

When both sides of an artwork are the same, it has symmetrical balance. If the sides are different, but feel equally important, it has asymmetrical balance. A third kind of balance is radial, which means that all the elements center around a single point, like the spokes of a wheel.

Symmetrical balance

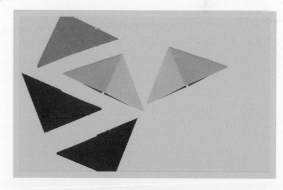

Asymmetrical balance

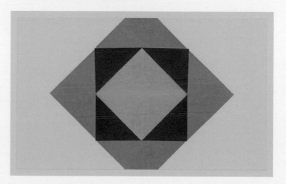

Radial balance

QUILLING

Quilling is an ancient way to make art by rolling up and pasting paper strips. It is called quilling because people first used bird feathers, or quills, to roll the paper around. Today, it is a popular way to make cards, decorations, signs, and even portraits of people.

You Will Need:

- Paper quilling strips or construction paper (variety of colors)
- Pencil and ruler
- Toothpick
- Scissors
- Clear glue
- Card stock or poster board

PROJECT GUIDES

1 If you have paper quilling strips, you can skip this step. Cut strips of paper ⅛-inch (.32 cm), ¼-inch (0.64 cm), or ½-inch (1.3 cm) wide. To do this, make marks on your paper on the top and bottom at intervals of the fraction you decide on. Then draw lines between the two marks and cut your strips with scissors.

2 Roll the paper around the end of a toothpick, or pencil. When you get to the end, let go of the coil a little to loosen it, and then slide it off the object you were using. You can keep it tight or unwind it a bit for a looser shape.

3 There are many shapes you can make from the coils by pinching the ends or unraveling part of the coil. For some shapes you may want to glue the end to the other part of the coil to keep it from unraveling. Make lots of different circles, both loose and tight.

4 Pinch some coils into eye shapes and squares.

5 Arrange your coils on a piece of card stock or poster board and then glue each coil in place by putting a small amount of glue on one edge.

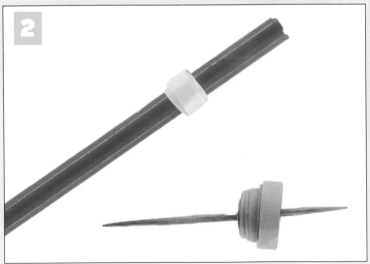

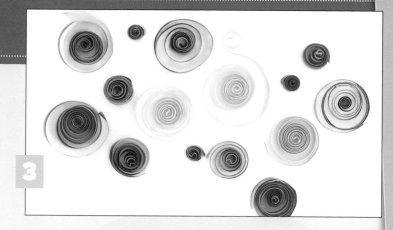

3

4

5

YULIA BRODSKAYA •••O

Russia/England

Yulia Brodskaya coils and shapes paper into colorful art. She started out by trying to spell out her name with paper. She says she didn't even know she was quilling! She doesn't need a lot of tools, just some heavy paper, a straw for curling it, toothpicks for making tighter circles, a ruler, glue, and scissors. She sometimes packs her paper strips so tightly that they look like the strokes of a paintbrush. It can take as long as five weeks for her to complete a quilled artwork.

FFlowers, 2016

When describing her paper artworks, Yulia Brodskaya says she is drawing with paper instead of on it.

15

MARBLING ART

Paper marbling has been practiced for centuries in Japan, Turkey, Iran, and India. From there, the technique spread worldwide. Paint, ink, food coloring, and even nail polish can be used for marbling! The colors are placed on water or some other liquid-like substance, then transferred to paper or fabric. It creates a pattern that looks like marble stone.

You Will Need:
- Cardboard
- Toothpicks
- Tape
- Tray
- Newspaper
- Shaving cream (foam)
- Acrylic craft paint (in bottles)
- Watercolor or heavy paper
- Plastic ruler

PROJECT GUIDES

1. Cut three pieces of cardboard. Make two tools for swirling paint by arranging toothpicks along one edge of the two pieces of cardboard. Tape the toothpicks in place.

2. Prepare your work area. Lay some newspaper out to work on. Put a tray on top of the newspaper. Cover the tray with shaving cream. Smooth the shaving cream out with the third piece of cardboard.

3. Hold a bottle of paint upside down. Drizzle paint over the shaving cream. Repeat with other colors of paint.

4. Swirl the paint with the tools you made in step one.

5. Lay a sheet of paper on top of the shaving cream. Press down all over with your hand so all of the paper comes in contact with the shaving cream.

6. Pull the paper out of the shaving cream. Lay it flat on the newspaper. Drag a ruler across the paper to remove the shaving cream.

7. Leave to dry.

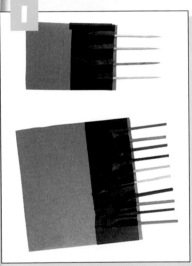

5

6

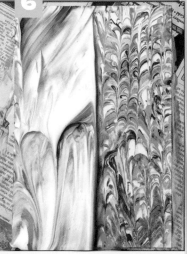

7

SUMINAGASHI

In Japan, people began marbling paper around the 1100s. Some art historians believe it first happend by accident! *Suminagashi*, the Japanese name for marbling, means spilled ink. In this technique, drops of ink are added to a bowl of still water. The ink drops expand to make a design. Artists blow on the drops or move them with a small brush or even a hair to get the look they want. Suminagashi artists often portray scenes of mountains, rivers, and oceans.

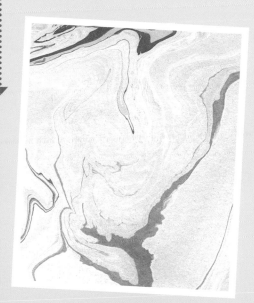

Tip

Follow steps three to seven again. The old colors will make an interesting background.

Try This!

Try the Japanese marbling technique. You will need a tray of water and marbling inks. These special inks are water-based and float on plain water. Drop ink into the water and swirl it. Carefully put the watercolor paper on top of the floating ink. Then lift it back out and leave it to dry.

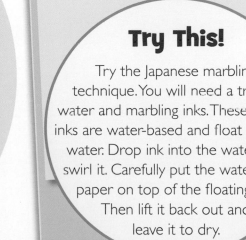

PAPER WEAVING

Use the technique of weaving to create a new piece of art from a discarded painting. Usually weaving is done with yarn, but it can be done with paper, too.

Create a paper weave with a **warp** and **weft**. The warp runs vertically, or up and down, and the weft runs horizontally, or from side to side. To weave, you move the weft strips of paper over and under the warp paper.

PROJECT GUIDES

1. Select a discarded painting that you would like to make into a new piece of art. Cut the painting in half.

2. In one half of the painting, use scissors to cut evenly spaced slits along the long side. Leave about a half-inch (1.3 cm) of the piece uncut on all sides. This will be your weft.

3. Use scissors to cut the other half of the painting into strips. Cut on the long side so that the strips are longer than the width of the weft. The strips can be thin or wide but should be all about the same width.

4. Start weaving the strips into the piece with slits. Slide the strip under the first slit and over the next slit. Repeat until you have reached the other side. Start weaving your next strip, but do the opposite, following an over-under pattern. Repeat this as you move down the painting.

5. As you fill up the piece with slits, keep pushing the pieces to the end so they are snug. Keep weaving until the slits are full of strips.

Slit

4

LARISSA NOWICKI

United States

Larissa Nowicki started out designing books about art, then began turning books into works of art! She collects old books that no one wants and slices up the pages. Then she weaves the strips back together into a design that expresses a feeling or idea. She uses the lines of the warp and weft to create both movement and texture.

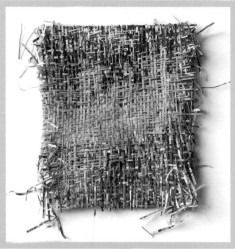

Succingere, 2018
Hand cut book pages, hand woven

5

PAPER MOSAIC

Mosaics are made from small pieces of paper, glass, stone, beads, shells, or other materials. The pieces are called tesserae. The word comes from ancient Greek. It means "four-sided," but they don't actually have to have four sides. In this exercise, you will create a mosaic effect using small pieces of card stock. To create the mosaic effect you do not overlap any pieces. Let the background show between every piece. In a real mosaic, this space would be filled with grout, which is a mixture of water, cement, and sand.

You Will Need:

- Card stock (variety of colors)
- Scissors
- Pencil
- Art board
- Brush
- Clear glue

Try This!

Abstract art often has no recognizable subject. You can create an abstract mosaic. Rather than a real-life subject, draw some shapes or spirals. Fill in the subject and background with different colors of paper squares.

PROJECT GUIDES

1 Use scissors to cut strips from a variety of colors of card stock.

2 Cut the strips into squares and rectangles. The shapes should be similar sizes.

3 On an art board or heavy piece of paper, draw a simple figure, like the bird in this example. Draw it slightly off-center to make the composition more interesting.

4 Brush glue over the bird sketch. Place card stock pieces on the glue and press down. You may have to cut some pieces to make them fit or fill in spaces. The beak is one square cut in half on a diagonal. Use different colors of card stock to make sections of the bird stand out. Continue adding more pieces until the bird is filled in.

5 To create a frame, brush glue around the outside edge. Place card stock pieces on the glue and press down. This will also help to create a sense of **unity** in your art.

6 Brush glue in the areas around the bird. Place card stock pieces on the glue and press down. Continue until you have filled in the whole background.

4

5

6

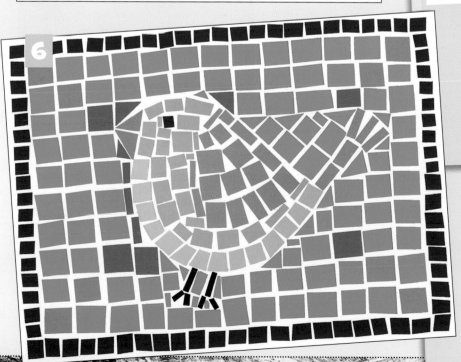

People have been making mosaics for thousands of years all over the world. Mosaics can be found on floors, ceilings, fountains, jewelry, and household objects. The images show how people dressed, what they ate, what pets they had, and how they worshiped. Mosaic-making remains a popular craft today for people of all ages, from school kids to professional artists.

Ancient Roman mosaic of a parrot, Seville, Spain.

Try This!

When you are finished, you can brush clear glue or Mod Podge over the colored pieces of card stock. This will make them shiny and look like tiles.

21

COLLAGE IT

Collage involves gluing pieces of different materials to a surface. The name comes from the French word *coller*, which means "to glue." Use small torn pieces of paper to "paint" an image. From a distance, you only see color but when you look up close, you see that it is something else.

You Will Need:

● Variety of papers, old magazines, and books
● Pencil
● Art board
● Brush
● Clear glue

PROJECT GUIDES

1 Draw the shape of a fish or other subject on the collage base so that you have a basic outline to use for your collage. Make it quite large so it can be the **focal point.**

2 Collect magazine and book pictures you would like to use. You can consider color and texture in your choices. Make sure to have different colors to create contrast in your collage. Very light pieces make good highlights, or bright spots.

3 To create the collage, you can start by tearing many small pieces. Leave some of the paper intact, you may need to tear some specific shapes to fill in areas of the collage later.

4 Fill in the background first. Brush glue on a section of background and then press torn pieces into the glue. Start from the bottom and work your way to the top. As you finish a section you can brush glue on top to help secure the pieces to the art board.

5 Start to fill in the subject. Overlap the pieces at the edges over the background.

6 Continue to fill in the subject. Tear smaller pieces to fill in the little areas. Some other areas may need specific shapes, such as a mouth and eye. Tear out those shapes and glue to the collage. You can glue tiny bits of dark-colored pieces to outline the subject and help it stand out from the background.

KRIS GROVER

United States

Kris Grover recycles all kinds of paper, even maps and sheet music, for her torn paper paintings. She loves to hike and gets inspiration from nature. Grover says it seems like the birds in her back yard are saying, "Paint me next!" Sometimes she uses plain paper, and other times she spatters or stamps it for a special effect.

Goldfinch Nest, 2019

Try This!

Another type of collage is to cut specific shapes out from magazine pages and interesting art papers. Sketch out a design on paper. Cut out shapes to match the drawing. Glue decorative paper to an art board or heavy paper to create a background. Apply glue to the back of the shapes and then press on to the background. You can overlap some shapes to create an illusion of space.

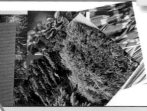

PAPER SCULPTURE

Construct a paper sculpture using a colorful abstract painting. In this exercise, you will be cutting and then twisting to create the **relief**. The texture of the painting adds visual interest to the artwork. It is up to you how far to take it. You can glue your sculpture to a base or leave it as a free-standing structure.

You Will Need:

- Watercolor or heavy drawing paper
- Watercolor paints
- Brush
- Scissors
- Tape
- Glue

PROJECT GUIDES

1 Use watercolor paint to paint an abstract painting. First, wet your paper completely. Then paint areas of color with a wet brush. Let the areas blend into each other. Add some splatter by loading a brush with a dark color of paint and tapping on the brush while holding it over the painting. Leave it to dry.

2 Cut slits into the paper. Cut holes out of the paper. Cut large fringes in the paper.

3 Start bending and folding the cut pieces of paper. Experiment to see what kind of shapes you can form.

4 Start gluing and taping pieces of the painting to each other to hold the form in place. Continue until you are happy with the way it looks. Look at it from above and the sides to see which way it should be displayed.

Try This!

Make several paper sculptures using this method. Paint a rectangular piece of cardboard to make a base. Let it dry. Use scissors to cut a piece of wire about the length of your forearm. Bend the wire in half. Push one end of the wire through one of the sculptures. Push the wire through the other sculptures. Poke the ends of the wire through the base. Bend the wire and tape it to the bottom of the base. Adjust the sculptures by bending them.

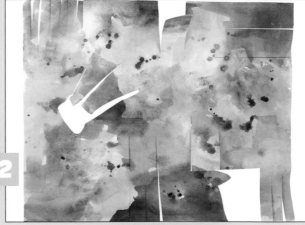

4

Try This!

1 Repeat step 1 from page 21, but make several paintings. Leave to dry.

2 Cut the paintings into a variety of different-sized strips.

3 Roll a strip around a pencil and secure with glue or tape. Slip the pencil out. Repeat with the other strips.

4 Paint a rectangular piece of cardboard to make a base. Let it dry.

5 Starting at the bottom, glue some tubes to the base. Glue more tubes to those tubes. Keep gluing more until you are out of tubes and you have assembled a 3-D sculpture.

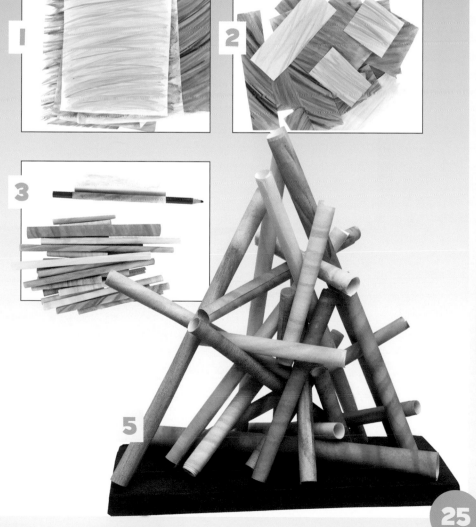

25

PAPER FLOWERS

Flowers and art go together naturally. Take a close look at some flowers. Notice how each petal looks like it has been hand painted. Look at the texture, shape, and form. Many artists over time have tried to capture the beauty of flowers in paintings. In this exercise, rather than paint a flower, you will reproduce a beautiful 3-D flower using paper.

You Will Need:
- Watercolor paper or heavy drawing paper
- Pencil
- Scissors
- Watercolor paint
- Brushes
- Craft wire
- Glue stick
- Green tape

PROJECT GUIDES

1 Cut a strip of paper 6 inches by 1.5 inches (15.25 cm by 3.8 cm) wide. Make a fringe by cutting the strip almost to the other edge. This will be the **stamen.**

2 Draw about four to eight petals for the flower. Cut out the petals.

3 Use watercolors to paint the stamen and the petals. Leave to dry.

4 Use scissors to cut a piece of wire about 12 inches (30.5 cm) long. Starting at one end, wrap green tape tightly around the wire until the entire wire is covered. This will be the stem.

5 Apply glue to the uncut portion of the stamen on the unpainted side. Roll the stamen tightly around the end of the wire. Wrap green tape around the bottom of the stamen to further secure it to the wire.

6 Take one petal and bend the narrow end. Press the bent end against the taped stamen. Wrap tape around the petal end. Repeat this for each petal.

7 Carefully pull the petals down and adjust them until they look good. Fluff the stamen out. Add some black paint to the inside middle of the stamen. Make more flowers by repeating the steps.

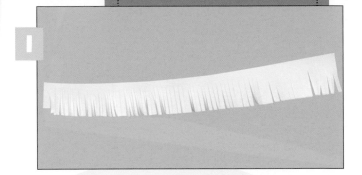

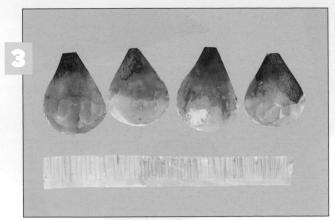

4

5

6

7

ANN WOOD

United States

When she was only 12 years old, Ann Wood was already painting flowers and birds on the walls of her bedroom. Today, she calls her artwork "drawing with scissors." She uses sharp embroidery scissors to sculpt her lifelike, yet magical, flowers and butterflies. She sometimes sews them by hand onto wool or velvet fabric that looks antique. To learn more about Ann's paper botanicals, explore @woodlucker on Instagram.

The image shows handmade paper flowers created in 2019.

PAPER MOBILE

Art doesn't need to be on the wall. A mobile is artwork with moving parts that hang from rods on wires or strings. The weight of the dangling objects is balanced so that the mobile doesn't tilt too much one way. Babies often have mobiles of animals over their cribs. In this exercise, you will create a beautiful mobile with birds dangling in the air.

You Will Need:

- Drawing paper
- Origami paper or construction paper
- Pencil
- Scissors
- Glue stick
- String or thread
- Tape
- Twig or dowel

PROJECT GUIDES

1. Cut a piece of drawing paper to be the same size as your origami paper. On the drawing paper, draw the side profile of a bird. Make sure the top of the bird runs along the top edge of the paper. Draw an outline of a wing and a beak also along an edge. Cut out the three pieces. These will be the pattern.

2. Fold a piece of the origami paper. Place a pattern piece on top. Line up the top of the pattern with the fold line. Cut around the pattern. Repeat for the other two pieces. Repeat to cut out five more birds.

3. Use a glue stick to glue the wings to the body of the bird. Glue the beak to the front of the bird.

4. Repeat for the rest of the birds.

5. Cut 24 small strips of paper from the scraps left from step 2. Roll them around a pencil to curl them. Glue four strips to the tail of each bird.

6. Cut six pieces of string about the length of your arm. Use scissors to make a tiny slit on each bird right behind the wing. Push one end of a string through the slit on each bird. Tape each string in place. Tie the other ends of the strings to a twig or dowel. (You can also tie your birds to two twigs that are tied together in an "X.") Tie another piece of string to the middle of your mobile to hang it.

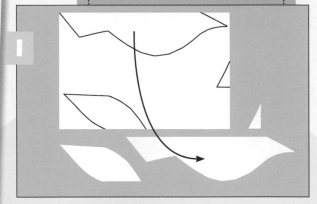

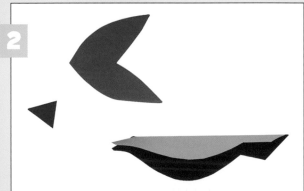

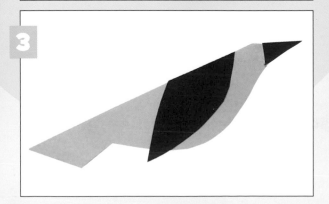

4

5

6

Try This!

Kirigami is a variation of origami. In kirigami, not only do you fold paper, you also cut it. After cutting a design, the paper is unfolded to reveal an amazing, interconnected design. Try the simple project below. If you like it, try more intricate folds and designs.

- Fold a piece of construction paper in half lengthwise. Tear it in half along the fold.

- Fold the half piece in half. Fold each half in half again.

- Unfold the paper. Fold the four sections accordion style.

- Draw a bird on a branch on the top. Part of the branch must touch the fold edge.

- Use scissors to cut around the drawing. Unfold the paper and you have four birds on a branch!

Books

Rosenberg, Chiharu. *Cut and Create Paper Mosaics: Craft Mosaic-by-Number Artworks with Paper Tiles, Scissors, and Glue.* Race Point Publishing, 2017.

Schwake, Susan and Schwake, Rainer. *Art Lab for Kids: 52 Creative Adventures in Drawing, Painting, Printmaking, Paper, and Mixed Media-For Budding Artists of All Ages.* Quarry Books, 2012.

Watt, Fiona. *Big Book of Papercraft.* Usborne, 2007

Woodley, Maggy. *Easy Paper Projects: 60 Crafts You Can Wear, Gift, Use and Admire.* Page Street Publishing, 2019.

Websites

National Gallery of Art

www.nga.gov/education/kids.html

NGAkids Art Zone includes descriptions of interactive art-making tools that are free to download. You can also explore the collection of the National Gallery.

Tate—A network of four art museums in the UK

www.tate.org.uk/kids

This website features a wonderful collection of quizzes, art activities to download, and videos.

Pics4Learning

www.pics4learning.com/

This website features a great collection of photos that students can use for classroom projects. The images are copyright-friendly. Includes a great selection of animal photos.

GLOSSARY

abstract art Art that can be made from lines, shapes, and colors that do not represent an actual form but convey emotion

composition The arrangement of all the shapes, lines, colors, and textures in an artwork

contrast The arrangement of opposite elements in art; for example, light and dark

focal point The area of an artwork that attracts the most attention and draws the viewer's eye

geometric Describing shapes, such as circles, triangles, or squares, that have perfect form and don't often appear in nature

line In art, the edge between two colors or shapes

mirror image An identical image, although reversed, such as a reflection in a mirror

negative space The space around and between subjects of an artwork or photo

organic Describing shapes and forms associated with the natural world and are not geometric

overlapping Placing so that part of one covers part of another

pattern A model to be followed

perpendicular At a right angle to a line or surface, like the lines of the letter L

positive space The space taken up by the main subject of an artwork or photo

relief A design that shows contrast between elements using line, color, and shading

shape Any enclosed space in an artwork

stamen The central part of a flower where pollen is produced

symmetry The qualities of balance, repetition, and harmony in an artwork

texture An element of art that conveys the surface quality of an object

three-dimensional (3-D) Objects have height, width, and depth, which are called dimensions. When an artwork has all three, it's called three-dimensional.

two-dimensional Having the two dimensions of length and width

unity The effect created when elements of an artwork combine to make the composition balanced and harmonious

warp Threads or strips that run vertically, or up and down

weft Threads or strips that run horizontally, or side to side

INDEX

ABOUT THE AUTHOR

Sandee Ewasiuk is a graduate of OCAD. She has participated in many group and solo exhibitions and her paintings can be found in corporate and private collections around the world. She currently divides her time between painting and teaching art at the Dundas Valley School of Art, The Art Gallery of Burlington, and Fleming College/Halliburton School of Art. She recently spent a month in Thailand as an artist-in-residence, exploring painting and mixed media. Sandee continues to experiment with and explore new ideas and techniques.